It brings me much pleasure to
be able to present to you this fine
selection of appealing cookie recipes.
While testing and sampling for this
compilation it became more and more
apparent that the options could
continue indefinitely; these recipes
are the choicest of the many tested.
I sincerely hope that this collection
will expand your repertoire of baking
to share with your family and friends.

Enjoy!

Gayle Hansen
B. H. Ec.
North Vancouver, B.C.
1984

Books in the 'Just Series'
over 100,000 in print

Just Muffins 1978

Just Casseroles 1981

Just for Tea 1982

Just Cookies 1984

Just Muffins
P.O. Box 86943
North Vancouver, BC
V7L 4P6

Printed by Cranbrook Litho Press Ltd.
Cranbrook, B.C.

Not to be reprinted without permission
of the author

© Gaye Hansen 1984
ISBN 0-9691644-3-2   Printed in Canada

Table of Contents

Drop Cookies

Neighbourhood Favourites

A great basic cookie and lots of variations

m.	Imp.	
250 gm	1 c	shortening
300 ml	1¼ c	brown sugar, packed lightly
1	1	egg
5 ml	1 t	vanilla
250 ml	1 c	flour
2 ml	½ t	baking powder
2 ml	½ t	baking soda
2 ml	½ t	salt
375 ml	1½ c	rolled oats
250 ml	1 c	coconut, shred or flake

Cream shortening and sugar, beat in egg and vanilla. Stir in flour, baking powder and baking soda, salt. Add oats and coconut and mix well. Drop by teaspoons onto lightly greased cookie sheet. Bake, remove to cooling rack

Variations

- instead of coconut use chocolate chips, raisins or a mixture

Bake: 180° (350°)

Time: 12-15 min

Yield: 4 dozen

-1-

Brown Sugar Cookies

m	Imp	
1	1	egg
250 ml	1 c	brown sugar, packed
5 ml	1 t	vanilla
125 ml	½ c	flour
1 ml	¼ t	baking soda
1 ml	¼ t	salt
375 ml	1½ c	chopped walnuts

Beat egg until very light and fluffy. Add sugar and vanilla; beat again. Stir in remaining ingredients. Drop by teaspoons onto greased and floured cookie sheet allowing room for spreading. Bake just until edges start to brown. Remove to cooling rack immediately.

Bake: 180° (350°)
Time: 8 min
Yield: 4 dozen

Butterscotch Crisps

m.	Imp.	
125 gm	½ c	shortening
125 ml	½ c	brown sugar, packed
92 gm	3 oz	package butterscotch pudding mix, regular
1	1	egg
250 ml	1 c	flour
125 ml	½ c	rolled oats
5 ml	1 t	baking soda
5 ml	1 t	cream of tartar

Cream together the shortening, brown sugar, pudding mix. Add egg and beat well. Blend in remaining ingredients. Drop by teaspoonfuls onto lightly greased cookie sheet, flatten with a fork dipped in flour. Bake.

Bake: 180° (350°)
Time: 12 min
Yield: 4 dozen

Peanut Butter Cookies

An especially good version of a classic

m.	Imp.	
250 ml	1 c	brown sugar, packed
250 ml	1 c	sugar
250 gm	1 c	shortening
250 ml	1 c	peanut butter, any style
2	2	eggs
5 ml	1 t	vanilla
500 ml	2 c	flour
10 ml	2 t	soda

Beat sugars, shortening and peanut butter until fluffy and well combined. Add eggs and vanilla; beat again. Stir in flour and soda. Drop by teaspoons or more if desired onto lightly greased cookie sheet. Flatten with a fork dipped in flour. Bake. Remove to cooling rack to cool.

Variations

- add up to 250 ml (1 c) Spanish peanuts and /or chocolate chip pieces for added flavour and interest

Bake: 180° (350°)
Time: 12-15 min
Yield: 6-7 dozen

- 4 -

Peanut Butter Surprises

m	Imp	
125 gm	½c	margarine
250 ml	1 c	smooth peanut butter
250 ml	1 c	brown sugar, packed
30 ml	2T	honey
2	2	eggs
250 ml	1 c	flour
5 ml	1t	baking powder
2 ml	½t	salt
5 ml	1 t	cinnamon
250 ml	1 c	chocolate chips
250 ml	1 c	butterscotch chips
250 ml	1 c	chopped peanuts

Cream margarine and peanut butter; beat in brown sugar, honey and eggs. Stir in dry ingredients and mix well. Fold in remaining ingredients. Drop by teaspoons onto ungreased cookie sheet.

Bake: 180° (350°)
Time: 15 min
Yield: 4 dozen

He Man Cookies

m	Imp	
250 ml	1 c	sugar
500 ml	2 c	flour
5 ml	1 t	salt
5 ml	1 t	baking soda
5 ml	1 t	cinnamon
5 ml	1 t	nutmeg
500 ml	2 c	rolled oats
250 ml	1 c	raisins
250 ml	1 c	walnuts
125 ml	½ c	milk
2	2	eggs
175 ml	¾ c	shortening, melted

Place all the ingredients in a large bowl in the given order. Mix well. Drop by rounded tablespoons or more onto lightly greased cookie sheet. Bake and remove to cooling racks.

These have to be made big to be good

Bake : 180° (350°)
Time : 15 - 20 min
Yield: 2 dozen

Rich Oat Cookies

m	Imp	
250 gm	1 c	margarine
250 gm	1 c	shortening
300 ml	1¼ c	brown sugar, packed
5 ml	1 t	baking soda
30 ml	2 T	boiling water
2 ml	½ t	vanilla
500 ml	2 c	flour, preferably cake and pastry flour
2 ml	½ t	salt
500 ml	2 c	rolled oats

Cream margarine and shortening. Beat in brown sugar, baking soda dissolved in boiling water, vanilla. Add flour, salt and oats; mix well. Drop by teaspoonfuls onto lightly greased cookie sheets. Flatten with a fork dipped in flour.

Variation: Poppy Seed Cookies

To the above recipe add:

60 ml	4 T	poppy seed
2 ml	½ t	mace

Bake: 180° (350°)
Time: 12-15 min
Yield: 7 dozen

Bran Crispies
Delicious and nutritious

m.	Imp.	
250 gm	1 c	margarine or butter
125 ml	½ c	brown sugar, packed
250 ml	1 c	sugar
2	2	eggs
5 ml	1 t	vanilla
500 ml	2 c	flour
2 ml	½ t	baking soda
2 ml	½ t	salt
500 ml	2 c	bran flakes cereal
250 ml	1 c	raisins

Cream margarine with sugars until light. Add eggs and vanilla and beat thoroughly. Add remaining ingredients and mix well. Drop by teaspoonfuls onto lightly greased cookie sheets.

Bake: 190° (375°)
Time: 12-15 min
Yield: 5 dozen

Molasses Spice Cookies

Sugar and spice and all things nice

m	Imp	
250 gm	1 c	butter, margarine or shortening
250 ml	1 c	sugar
2	2	eggs
50 ml	¼ c	molasses
500 ml	2 c	flour
10 ml	2 t	baking soda
dash	dash	salt
5 ml	1 t	cinnamon
5 ml	1 t	cloves
5 ml	1 t	ginger
		icing sugar

Cream butter and sugar; beat in eggs and molasses. Stir in flour, soda, salt and spices. Drop by teaspoons onto lightly greased cookie sheet. Bake. Remove to cooling rack. Cool completely. Dust with icing sugar.

Bake: 190° (375°)
Time: 10-12 min
Yield: 3 dozen

Golden Crisps

A crisp cookie that goes well with all ocassions

m	Imp	
250 gm	1 c	margarine
250 ml	1 c	sugar
22 ml	1½ T	milk
15 ml	1 T	Roger's golden syrup
5 ml	1 t	baking soda
500 ml	2 c	flour

Cream margarine and sugar until light. Heat milk and syrup and stir in baking soda. Add to sugar mixture and blend. Stir in flour. Drop by teaspoons onto lightly greased baking sheets. Flatten with a fork dipped in flour.

Bake: 180° (350°)
Time: 10-12 min
Yield: 5 dozen

Elephant's Ears
Wonderfully spiced and yummy

m.	Imp.	
125 gm	½ c	margarine
175 gm	¾ c	shortening or lard
750 ml	3 c	sugar
75 ml	⅓ c	liquid honey or syrup
2	2	eggs
625 ml	2½ c	rolled oats
750 ml	3 c	flour
20 ml	4 t	baking soda
5 ml	1 t	salt
5 ml	1 t	allspice
10 ml	2 t	ginger
5 ml	1 t	cinnamon
250 ml	1 c	raisins, walnuts, poppy seed, sesame seed, sunflower seed in any combination

Combine the ingredients in the given order. Roll into balls and flatten with a fork dipped in flour. Bake.

Bake: 190° (375°)
Time: 10-12 min
Yield: 6-7 dozen

Almond Cookies

m	Imp	
125 gm	½c	margarine or shortening
125 ml	½c	sugar
1	1	egg
1 ml	¼t	lemon extract
300 ml	1¼c	flour
1 ml	¼t	baking powder
1 ml	¼t	salt
125 ml	½c	chopped blanched almonds
		blanched almond halves

Cream margarine or shortening, sugar, egg and lemon extract. Stir in flour, baking powder, salt and almonds. Mix well. Drop by teaspoons onto lightly greased cookie sheet. Press an almond half onto each cookie. Bake. Remove to cooling racks.

Bake: 180° (350°)
Time: 15 min
Yield: 3 dozen

Raisin Cookies

A soft cookie full of nuts, raisins and spices

m	Imp	
125 gm	½c	shortening
500 ml	2 c	brown sugar, packed
2	2	eggs
250 ml	1 c	evaporated milk, undiluted
15 ml	1T	vinegar
500 ml	2c	flour
5 ml	1t	baking soda
2 ml	½t	salt
5 ml	1 t	cinnamon
5 ml	1 t	cloves
5 ml	1 t	allspice
1 ml	¼t	nutmeg
750 ml	3 c	raisins
250 ml	1 c	chopped nuts

Beat shortening, sugar and eggs until light. Blend in evaporated milk combined with vinegar. Stir in dry ingredients, raisins and nuts. Drop by rounded teaspoonfuls onto lightly greased cookie sheet.

Bake: 180° (350°)
Time: 15 min
Yield: 6 dozen

Chocolate Chip Cookies (Toll House Cookies)

m.	Imp.	
250 gm	1 c	butter or margarine
175 ml	3/4 c	sugar
175 ml	3/4 c	brown sugar, packed
2	2	eggs
5 ml	1 t	vanilla
550 ml	2 1/4 c	flour
5 ml	1 t	soda
5 ml	1 t	salt
250 ml	1 c	chopped walnuts
250-500 ml	1-2 c	chocolate chips

Cream butter and sugars until light. Add eggs and vanilla and beat well. Add remaining ingredients and mix thoroughly. Drop by teaspoons onto lightly greased cookie sheet. Bake and remove to cooling rack.

Variations

- use mint chips or butterscotch pieces in place of chocolate
- add 50 ml (1/4 c) chopped maraschino cherries or coconut
- add 250 ml (1 c) rolled oats plus an additional 50 ml (1/4 c) brown sugar
- try carob chips   Bake: 180° (350°)

Time: 10-12 min

Yield: 8 dozen

Coconut Cookies

Coconut lovers will be delighted with these

m	Imp	
250 gm	1c	butter or margarine
250 ml	1c	icing sugar
50 ml	1/4 c	sugar
1	1	egg
5 ml	1t	vanilla
500 ml	2c	flour
625 ml	2½ c	coconut, flaked

Cream butter and sugars; beat in egg and vanilla. Stir in flour and coconut. Drop by teaspoons onto lightly greased cookie sheet. Flatten with a floured fork. Bake, watching carefully for over browning

If you like a more uniform cookie form into 2½ cm (1") balls before flattening.

Bake: 160° (325°)
Time: 8 min
Yield: 5 dozen

Orange Drops

Large orange flavoured cookies with
a cake-like texture

m	Imp	
150 gm	2/3 c	butter or margarine
250 ml	1 c	sugar
2	2	eggs
125 ml	1/2 c	orange juice
15 ml	1T	grated orange rind
550 ml	2 1/4 c	flour
2 ml	1/2 t	salt
2 ml	1/2 t	baking soda
125 ml	1/2 c	coarsely chopped walnuts

Cream butter, sugar; beat in
eggs, orange juice and rind. Stir in
dry ingredients; fold in nuts. Drop by
heaping teaspoons onto greased cookie
sheet. Bake; cool on a rack. Swirl with
the following frosting covering tops
completely

Frosting: blend until smooth

375 ml	1 1/2 c	icing sugar
45 ml	3T	butter or margarine
25 ml	1 1/2 T	orange juice
10 ml	2 t	grated orange rind

Bake: 180° (350°)
Time: 10 min
Yield: 3 dozen

Jubilee Jumbles

m	Imp	
125 gm	1/2 c	shortening or margarine
375 ml	1 1/2 c	brown sugar, packed
2	2	eggs
250 ml	1 c	sour cream
5 ml	1 t	vanilla
675 ml	2 3/4 c	flour
2 ml	1/2 t	baking soda
5 ml	1 t	salt
250 ml	1 c	chopped walnuts

Cream shortening, sugar and eggs; beat in sour cream and vanilla. Stir in dry ingredients; mix in nuts. Drop by teaspoons onto lightly greased cookie sheet. Frost while slightly warm

Glaze

m	Imp	
125 gm	1/2 c	butter or margarine melted
500 gm	2 c	icing sugar
5 ml	1 t	vanilla
10-20 ml	2-4 t	hot water

Blend until smooth and a good spreading consistency

Variation: try a creamy orange frosting instead of glaze. See page 16

Bake: 190° (375°)
Time: 10-12 min
Yield: 5 dozen

Florentines

m	Imp	
250 ml	1 c	sliced almonds
125 ml	½ c	candied orange peel or fruit mix, chopped
50 ml	¼ c	diced candied or maraschino cherries
5 ml	1 t	grated lemon rind
50 ml	¼ c	flour
50 ml	¼ c	butter or margarine
50 ml	¼ c	sugar
50 ml	¼ c	honey
50 ml	¼ c	heavy cream

Combine almonds, fruits and flour in a small bowl; toss to coat evenly. Combine remaining ingredients in a small saucepan. Heat slowly with stirring until mixture bubbles. Remove from heat; stir in almond mixture just until well coated. Drop by teaspoons onto greased cookie sheet and spread thin with a spatula to 4 cm (1½"). Bake; cool 1 minute, turn over to flat side up to cool completely. Spread chocolate coating thinly on flat side almost to edges. Serve chocolate side down.

Chocolate coating

	12 squares semisweet chocolate
45 ml	3 T margarine

Melt over hot water

Bake: 180° (350°)
Time: 10 min
Yield: 5 dozen

— 18 —

Cookies!

These crispy cookies are bound to become family favourites

m	Imp	
250 gm	1c	margarine or shortening
250 ml	1c	sugar
1	1	egg
625 ml	2½c	flour
10 ml	2 t	cream of tartar
5 ml	1 t	baking soda

Cream margarine and sugar. Beat in egg. Stir in flour, cream of tartar and baking soda. Form into 2½ cm (1") balls and flatten with floured fork. Bake. Cool on racks.

Note:

Sound like too much cream of tartar? It's no mistake, the cream of tartar is what makes these so crispy. Various ingredients such as peanuts, walnuts, raisins, cherries etc. may be added but they make an excellent plain cookie.

Bake: 180° (350°)
Time: 12 min
Yield: 5 dozen

Basic Butter Cookies

A very tender delicate cookie with
a multitude of variations

m.	Imp.	
250 ml	1 c	flour
125 ml	1/2 c	cornstarch
125 ml	1/2 c	icing sugar
175 gm	3/4 c	butter
125 ml	1/2 c	coarsely chopped walnuts

Stir dry ingredients together in a
large bowl. Add butter and mix well.
Stir in walnuts. Drop by teaspoons
onto lightly greased cookie sheet.
Bake until lightly golden.

Variations

Instead of walnuts use one of
the following:

    chocolate chips
    toasted coconut
    raisins
    chopped dates
    pecans
    granola

Bake: 150° (300°)
Time: 25 min
Yield: about 30

Chocolate Orange Drops
Something unusual for special times

m	Imp	
125 gm	½ c	butter
125 gm	3 oz	cream cheese, softened
125 ml	½ c	icing sugar
1	1	egg
15 ml	1 T	grated orange rind
5 ml	1 t	vanilla
250 ml	1 c	flour
2 ml	½ t	salt
250 ml	1 c	chocolate chips

Beat butter and cream cheese until light and fluffy. Add sugar and egg and beat until smooth. Blend in orange rind and vanilla. Stir in flour and salt; fold in chocolate chips. Drop by teaspoons onto lightly greased cookie sheet.

Bake: 180° (350°)
Time: 15-20 min
Yield: 4 dozen

O Henry's Cookies

Needless to say, these don't last long

m	Imp	
125 gm	1/2 c	butter or margarine
175 ml	3/4 c	sugar
1	1	egg
2 ml	1/2 t	vanilla
325 ml	1 1/3 c	flour
2 ml	1/2 t	baking soda
2 ml	1/2 t	salt
2-40 gm	2	O Henry bars

Cream butter and sugar; beat in egg and vanilla. Stir in flour, baking soda and salt. Slice bars into 1/2 cm (1/4") slices and chop coarsely. Add to cookie mixture and stir in. Drop by teaspoons onto lightly greased cookie sheet. Bake. Remove immediately to cooling racks before melted caramel hardens.

Bake: 180° (350°)
Time: 15 min
Yield: 4 dozen

Porcupines
A no-bake cookie

m	Imp	
250 ml	1c	chocolate chips
250 ml	1c	butterscotch chips
250 ml	1c	peanuts, salted or unsalted
250 ml	1c	chow mein noodles

Melt chocolate and butterscotch chips over hot water. Remove from heat and gently fold in peanuts and noodles. Drop by small teaspoonfuls onto wax paper. Refrigerate to set. Store in covered container in the refrigerator or may be frozen.

Variations
- use half peanuts and half raisins
- replace a small portion 75 ml (⅓ c) of chocolate chips using mint flavoured chips

Yield: 3 dozen

Benne Wafers

Benne, an African word, means sesame

m.	Imp.	
125 ml	½ c	sesame seed
250 gm	1 c	butter or margarine
150 ml	⅔ c	sugar
1 ml	¼ t	salt
15 ml	1 T	milk
2 ml	½ t	almond or vanilla extract
400 ml	1⅔ c	flour

Toast sesame seeds in 180°(350°) oven until golden. Cream butter and sugar until light. Add remaining ingredients and sesame seeds; mix well. Drop by teaspoonfuls onto lightly greased cookie sheet. Flatten with a fork dipped in flour.

Bake: 180° (350°)
Time: 15 min.
Yield: 4 dozen

Mudpies

A double chocolate treat

m	Imp	
125 gm	½ c	margarine
250 ml	1 c	sugar
2	2	eggs
15 ml	3 t	vanilla
3	3	squares unsweetened chocolate, melted
250 ml	1 c	flour
2 ml	½ t	baking powder
5 ml	1 t	salt
500 ml	2 c	chopped walnuts
250 ml	1 c	chocolate chips

Cream margarine and sugar; beat in eggs, vanilla and melted chocolate. Blend well. Stir in remaining ingredients. Drop by tablespoons onto lightly greased cookie sheet or smaller teaspoonfuls if desired.

Bake: 180° (350°)
Time: 15 min
Yield: about 30

Grandaddies
A healthy oat and raisin cookie

m.	Imp.	
175 gm	3/4 c	margarine
350 ml	1 1/2 c	brown sugar, lightly packed
2	2	eggs
5 ml	1 t	vanilla
250 ml	1 c	flour
5 ml	1 t	soda
2 ml	1/2 t	salt
500 ml	2 c	rolled oats
50 ml	1/4 c	wheat germ
175 ml	3/4 c	coconut
175 ml	3/4 c	raisins
125 ml	1/2 c	chocolate chips
125 ml	1/2 c	chopped walnuts

Cream margarine, brown sugar, eggs and vanilla thoroughly. Add flour, soda, salt, oats and wheatgerm. Mix well. Stir in remaining ingredients. Drop by tablespoonfuls onto lightly greased cookie sheets. Flatten with a floured fork. Bake until golden.

Bake: 180° (350°)
Time: 15 min.
Yield: 3 dozen

Melting Moments
Tender, dainty morsels

m	Imp	
125 gm	½ c	butter or margarine
250 ml	1 c	flour
15 ml	1T	icing sugar

Combine ingredients thoroughly. Drop by scant teaspoons onto lightly greased cookie sheets. Bake and cool. Sandwich with one of the following icings:

Tinted Icing

125 ml	½ c	icing sugar
7 ml	1½ t	milk
15 ml	1T	butter
2	2	drops food coloring

Orange Icing

125 ml	½ c	icing sugar
7 ml	1½ t	orange juice
2 ml	½ t	orange rind
15 ml	1T	butter

Combine icing ingredients thoroughly.

Bake: 160° (325°)
Time: 15 - 18 min
Yield: 2 dozen

Moon before the Mist

These have no eggs or milk - a plus
for those with allergies

m	Imp	
250 ml	1 c	raisins
125 ml	½ c	raisin juice
5 ml	1 t	instant coffee powder
125 gm	½ c	butter or margarine
125 ml	½ c	sugar
500 ml	2 c	flour
1 ml	¼ t	salt
5 ml	1 t	soda
1 ml	¼ t	cloves
1 ml	¼ t	cinnamon

Boil raisins in 175 ml (3/4 c) water.
Drain, reserve 125 ml (½ c) of the juice.
Add coffee powder to juice, stir. Cool.
Cream butter and sugar thoroughly. Add
dry ingredients, raisins and juice.
Mix well. Drop by teaspoonfuls onto
lightly greased cookie sheet.

Bake: 180° (350°)
Time: 10-15 min
Yield: 3 dozen

Vanilla Sand Cookies

A simple but effective cookie
suitable for any occasion

m	Imp	
375 gm	1½ c	butter
750 ml	3 c	flour
175 ml	3/4 c	sugar
5 ml	1 t	vanilla
150 ml	2/3 c	blanched, finely ground almonds

Work all the ingredients together until you have a stiff dough; use your hands if necessary. Form into balls 2½ cm (1") and flatten to make a circle with cracked edges

Create unusual designs by using
- a cookie stamp
- a meat pounder to make a waffle effect or ridges depending on the mallet
- a potato masher
- a decorative glass bottom

Bake: 160° (325°)
Time: 25 min
Yield: 4 dozen

Bird's Nests

Also known as Thimble Cookies or
Swedish Thumbprints

m	Imp	
125 gm	1/2 c	butter or margarine
50 ml	1/4 c	brown sugar, packed
1	1	egg yolk
250 ml	1 c	flour
1	1	egg white, slightly beaten
125 ml	1/2 c	finely chopped walnuts
		strawberry jam

Cream butter and sugar; beat in
egg yolk. Stir in flour. Form into 2 1/2 cm
(1") balls; dip into egg white to coat;
roll in nuts. Place on ungreased cookie
sheet; press centres with thimble or
thumb. Bake 5 minutes and press
hole again. Bake a further 10 minutes
or until done. Cool. Fill with straw-
berry jam. (Freeze before filling for
long time keeping)
Roll in finely crushed cornflakes if you prefer

Bake: 180° (350°)
Time: 15 min.
Yield: 2 dozen

Chocolate Thumbprints

A chocolate version of Bird's Nests

m	Imp	
125 gm	½ c	butter or margarine
28 gm	1-oz	square unsweetened chocolate, melted
125 ml	½ c	sugar
1	1	egg yolk
1 ml	¼ t	vanilla
250 ml	1 c	flour
1 ml	¼ t	salt
1	1	egg white, slightly beaten
175 ml	¾ c	finely chopped walnuts
75 ml	⅓ c	chocolate chips

Cream butter; add melted chocolate. Add sugar, egg yolk and vanilla, mix thoroughly. Stir in flour and salt. Form into 2½ cm (1") balls, dip into egg white to coat; roll in nuts. Place on ungreased cookie sheet, press thumb gently in centre of each. Bake. Place 4 or 5 chocolate chips into thumbprint, return to oven 1 minute Spread chocolate evenly over thumbprint.

Bake: 180° (350°)

Time: 12-15 min

Yield: 3 dozen

Pecan Kisses

Also known as Snowballs or
Swedish Butterballs

m	Imp	
250 gm	1c	butter
125 ml	½c	icing sugar
5 ml	1t	vanilla
625 ml	2½c	cake and pastry flour (use 50 ml, ¼c. less for all purpose flour)
250 ml	1c	finely chopped pecans
		icing sugar

Cream butter, icing sugar and vanilla thoroughly. Add flour, mix well. Stir in pecans. Form into 2½ cm (1") balls. Place on ungreased cookie sheet. Bake. Cool completely and dust with icing sugar

Variations

walnuts may replace pecans

Bake: 200° (400°)
Time: 8-12 min
Yield: 4 dozen

Cherry Snowballs

Cherries wrapped in an almond pastry make wonderful Christmas fancies

m	Imp	
250 gm	1 c	butter or margarine
50 ml	¼ c	icing sugar
1 ml	¼ t	salt
5 ml	1 t	vanilla
500 ml	2 c	flour
250 ml	1 c	very finely chopped almonds
48	48	candied cherries
		icing sugar

Cream butter and sugar; stir in salt, vanilla, flour and almonds. Mix. Take a teaspoonful of dough, roll into a ball and flatten in the palm of your hand. Place a cherry in the centre and wrap dough over cherry to cover completely. Place on cookie sheet and bake. Cool completely and then dust with icing sugar.

Bake: 160° (325°)
Time: 35 min
Yield: 4 dozen

Plantation Cookies

These will flatten as they bake

m	Imp	
175 gm	¾ c	butter or margarine
250 ml	1 c	sugar
1	1	egg
75 ml	⅓ c	molasses
125 ml	½ c	chopped peanuts, salted or unsalted
500 ml	2 c	flour
10 ml	2 t	baking soda
5 ml	1 t	cinnamon
2 ml	½ t	cloves
2 ml	½ t	ginger
2 ml	½ t	nutmeg
1 ml	¼ t	salt
125 ml	½ c	finely chopped peanuts
50 ml	¼ c	sugar

Beat butter, sugar, egg and molasses. Add peanuts, flour, baking soda, spices and salt. Form into balls the size of a ping-pong ball; roll into combined peanuts and sugar. Place on lightly greased cookie sheet

Bake: 180° (350°)
Time: 15 min
Yield: 2 dozen

Cereal Snaps

m	Imp	
125 gm	½ c	butter or margarine
125 ml	½ c	brown sugar, packed
125 ml	½ c	sugar
1	1	egg
5 ml	1 t	vanilla
300 ml	1¼ c	flour
2 ml	½ t	baking powder
2 ml	½ t	baking soda
2 ml	½ t	salt
500 ml	2 c	crisp rice cereal
300 ml	1¼ c	flaked coconut

Cream butter with sugars; beat in egg and vanilla. Stir in dry ingredients and lastly cereal and coconut. Shape into 2 cm (3/4") balls, place on ungreased cookie sheet Bake; cool slightly and remove from pan.

Bake: 180° (350°)
Time: 10 min
Yield: 5 dozen

Choconut Dainties

The tips of these small rolls are dipped in chocolate to make an appealing cookie

m	Imp	
175 gm	3/4 c	margarine
175 ml	3/4 c	sugar
1	1	egg
7 ml	1½ t	vanilla
550 ml	2¼ c	flour
2 ml	½ t	salt
250 ml	1 c	chocolate chips

Cream margarine and sugar; beat in egg and vanilla. Stir in remaining ingredients and mix well. Shape into logs 5 cm x 1½ cm (2" x ½") Place on ungreased cookie sheet. Bake. Cool on wire racks. Dip ends of cookies into chocolate coating; roll ends in finely chopped walnuts, about 500 ml (2c)

Chocolate Coating

8	8	squares semisweet chocolate
30 ml	2T	margarine

Melt over hot water

Bake: 180° (350°)
Time: 15 min
Yield: 5 dozen

Delicious Dad's Cookies

Make these large or small depending on your family's appetites

m	Imp	
125 gm	½ c	shortening
125 gm	½ c	margarine
250 ml	l c	brown sugar, packed
250 ml	l c	sugar
2	2	eggs
5 ml	l t	vanilla
5 ml	l t	almond extract
425 ml	1 ¾ c	flour
5 ml	l t	baking powder
5 ml	l t	soda
2 ml	½ t	salt
2 ml	½ t	nutmeg
l ml	¼ t	cloves
500 ml	2 c	shredded or flaked coconut
250 ml	l c	chopped walnuts
500 ml	2 c	rolled oats

Cream shortening, margarine, sugars, eggs and extracts. Stir in remaining ingredients and mix well. Form into balls, place on greased sheet and flatten with fork. Bake: 190° (375°)

Time: 15 min

Yield: 4-6 dozen

Walnut Frosties
A self-frosting cookie!

m	Imp	
250 ml	1 c	brown sugar, packed
125 gm	½ c	butter or margarine
1	1	egg
5 ml	1 t	vanilla
425 ml	1¾ c	flour
2 ml	½ t	baking soda
250 ml	1 c	chopped walnuts
125 ml	½ c	brown sugar, packed
50 ml	¼ c	sour cream

Cream butter and sugar. Beat in egg and vanilla until light. Stir in flour and baking soda. Form into 2½ cm (1") balls and place on lightly greased cookie sheet. Make a generous sized thumb print in each; fill with a teaspoonful of the walnuts brown sugar and sour cream which have been well combined.

Bake: 180° (350°)
Time: 10-15 min
Yield: 3 dozen

Stamp Cookies
Lovely in their simplicity

m	Imp	
250 gm	1c	butter
125 ml	1/2c	sugar
5 ml	1t	vanilla
500 ml	2c	flour
2 ml	1/4t	salt
	sugar	

Cream butter and sugar, add vanilla and mix well. Stir in flour and salt. Chill dough. Form into 2 1/2 cm (1") balls and roll in sugar. Stamp with a cookie stamp*. Bake.

* bottom of a glass may be used, or flattened with a fork

Bake: 180° (350°)
Time: 12-15 min
Yield: 3 dozen

Turtles

m	Imp	
125 gm	½ c	butter or margarine
125 ml	½ c	brown sugar, packed
1	1	egg
1	1	egg yolk
1 ml	¼ t	vanilla
375 ml	1½ c	flour
1 ml	¼ t	baking soda
2 ml	½ t	salt
		pecan halves
1	1	egg white, unbeaten

Cream butter and brown sugar; beat in 1 egg, 1 egg yolk and vanilla. Add dry ingredients; mix well. Arrange pecan halves in groups of 3 to 5 on ungreased cookie sheet to resemble head and legs of turtle. Form dough into 2½ cm (1") balls; dip bottom of each into egg white and press lightly onto nuts letting tips of nuts show. Bake, cool and frost.

Chocolate Frosting

2	2	squares unsweetened chocolate
50 ml	¼ c	milk
15 ml	1 T	butter
250 ml	1 c	icing sugar, sifted

Cook chocolate, milk, butter over hot water until smooth. Remove from heat, beat in sugar until smooth

Bake: 180° (350°
Time: 12 min
Yield: 30

—40—

Oat Crisps

m.	Imp.	
150 gm	2/3 c	butter or margarine
125 ml	1/2 c	sugar
500 ml	2 c	rolled oats
250 ml	1 c	flake coconut
2 ml	1/2 t	cinnamon
5 ml	1 t	vanilla
5 ml	1 t	lemon rind
5 ml	1 t	orange rind
2 ml	1/2 t	salt

Cream butter and sugar. Add remaining ingredients and mix well. Form into a long roll 2-3 cm. diameter (about 1 inch). Wrap in wax paper and chill. Cut into slices and place on slightly greased cookie sheet. Bake and cool before removing from pan.

Bake: 160° (325°)
Time: 15-20 min.
Yield: 2 dozen

Butterscotch Cookies

m	Imp	
125 gm	½ c	butter or margarine
250 ml	1 c	brown sugar
1	1	egg
5 ml	1 t	vanilla
375 ml	1½ c	flour
2 ml	½ t	salt
2 ml	½ t	baking powder
1 ml	¼ t	baking soda
125 ml	½ c	chopped walnuts
125 ml	½ c	raisins

Cream butter and sugar; beat in egg and vanilla. Add remaining ingredients and mix well. Form into one large roll 7cm (about 3") wrap and chill several hours. Slice and bake on lightly greased cookie sheet.

Bake: 200° (400°)
Time: 8 min
Yield: 3 dozen

Cinnamon Slices

M	Imp	
550 ml	2¼ c	flour
125 ml	½ c	sugar
250 gm	1 c	butter or margarine
1	1	egg yolk
1	1	egg white, slightly beaten
45 ml	3 T	brown sugar, packed
5 ml	1 t	cinnamon

Stir flour and sugar together; cut in butter as for pastry. Add egg yolk and stir to combine. Form into 5 cm (2") diameter log. Brush with egg white and roll in brown sugar combined with cinnamon. Wrap and chill. Slice into ½ cm (¼") rounds and place on lightly greased cookie sheet. Bake; cool on racks

Bake: 180° (350°)
Time: 12-15 min
Yield: 4 dozen

Nut Edged Butter Rounds
These are definitely special

m	Imp	
125 gm	½ c	butter or margarine
150 ml	2/3 c	sugar
1	1	egg yolk
30 ml	2 T	light cream
375 ml	1½ c	flour
10 ml	2 t	baking powder
2 ml	½ t	salt
1	1	egg white, slightly beaten
75 ml	1/3 c	toasted almonds, finely chopped
45 ml	3 T	sugar

Cream butter and sugar. Beat in egg yolk and cream. Stir in flour, baking powder and salt. Form into one long roll 3½ cm (1½") diameter. Brush with egg white and roll in almonds combined with sugar. Wrap and chill several hours. Slice ½ cm (¼"). Place on lightly greased cookie sheet.

Bake: 200° (400°)
Time: 8-10 min
Yield: 4 dozen

Anise Seed Cookies

Anise has an unmistakable licorice flavor. These cookies are very crisp and keep well

m	Imp	
125 gm	½ c	butter
250 ml	1 c	sugar
1	1	egg
2 ml	½ t	vanilla
425 ml	1¾ c	flour
2 ml	½ t	salt
7 ml	1½ t	baking powder
7 ml	1½ t	anise seed

Cream butter and sugar; beat in egg and vanilla. Add remaining ingredients and mix well. Form into a roll; wrap and chill. Cut into thin slices. Place on lightly greased cookie sheet.

Bake: 200° (400°)
Time: 8 min
Yield: 5 dozen

Santa's Whiskers

A whimsical name for a very
appealing cookie

m	Imp	
250 gm	1c	butter or margarine
250 ml	1c	sugar
5 ml	1t	almond extract
625 ml	2½c	flour
175 ml	3/4c	maraschino cherries chopped finely
125 ml	½ c	pecans, chopped
175 ml	3/4c	coconut, flaked

Cream butter, sugar and extract.
Stir in flour, cherries and pecans.
Form into two rolls 5cm (2") diameter
Roll in coconut. Wrap and chill
several hours or overnight. Slice
½ cm (¼") thick and place on
ungreased cookie sheet.

Bake: 190 (375°)
Time: 12 min
Yield: 5 dozen

Rum and Butter Crisps

m	Imp	
250 gm	1 c	butter or margarine
250 ml	1 c	sugar
250 ml	1 c	brown sugar, packed lightly
7 ml	1½ t	rum extract
1	1	egg
30 ml	2 T	water
550 ml	2¼ c	flour
2 ml	½ t	baking soda
2 ml	½ t	salt
250 ml	1 c	chopped pecans

Cream butter, sugars, extract. Add egg, water and beat until light. Stir in remaining ingredients and mix well. Shape dough into 2 logs 5 cm (2") in diameter. Chill several hours. Cut into scant ½ cm (⅛") slices and place on lightly greased cookie sheets.

Bake: 200° (400°)
Time: 5-7 min
Yield: 5 dozen

Giant Oat Cookies

Enormous oat and raisin cookies

m	Imp	
375 ml	1½ c	raisins
2	2	eggs
250 gm	1 c	shortening
175 ml	¾ c	sugar
325 ml	1⅓ c	brown sugar, packed
30 ml	2 T	water
7 ml	1½ t	vanilla
500 ml	2 c	flour
5 ml	1 t	salt
2 ml	½ t	baking soda
10 ml	2 t	baking powder
900 ml	3 ¾ c	rolled oats

Cover raisins in hot water for 10 minutes; drain thoroughly. Cream eggs, shortening, sugars, water and vanilla. Stir in raisins and remaining ingredients. Form into 5 cm (2") rolls; wrap and chill until firm. Slice into 1½ cm (½") slices; place on baking sheets, lightly greased. Flatten to ½ cm (¼") and bake.

Bake: 190° (375°)
Time: 12-15 min
Yield: 3 dozen

Shortbread
M·m·m melt in your mouth goodness

m	Imp	
454 gm	1 pound	butter
250 ml	1 c	sugar
750 ml	3 c	flour
125 ml	½ c	rice flour

Cream butter until very whipped. Add sugar and beat until very light. Combine flours and gradually add to butter mixture. Knead gently with hands a few times. Roll out 3/4 cm (⅓") on a lightly floured surface. Cut into 5 cm (2") rounds. Place on ungreased cookie sheet.

Bake: 160° (325°)
Time: 20 min
Yield: 5 dozen

Canadian Oat Cakes

Excellent with cheeses and/or preserves

m	Imp	
375 ml	1½ c	rolled oats preferably large flake (or a combination of oats, rye barley, wheat)
30 ml	2 T	wheat germ
375 ml	1½ c	flour
125 ml	½ c	sugar
5 ml	1 t	salt
2 ml	½ t	baking soda
175 gm	3/4 c	lard
95 ml	3/8 c	cold water
		rolled oats

Stir dry ingredients together. Cut in lard until very fine. Add water to moisten. Roll very thin on a lightly floured surface; cut into squares 4 cm (1½"). Transfer squares to a surface liberally sprinkled with rolled oats. Sprinkle more oats on top and roll even thinner. Place on ungreased cookie sheet.

Bake: 180° (350°)
Time: 12 min
Yield: 9 dozen

Old Fashioned Sugar Cookies

The addition of orange make these unique.

M.	Imp.	
150 gm	2/3 c	shortening
300 ml	1 1/4 c	sugar
2	2	eggs
15 ml	1 T	orange juice
15 ml	1 T	grated orange rind
750 ml	3 c	flour
7 ml	1 1/2 t	salt
10 ml	2 t	baking powder

Cream shortening and sugar, beat in eggs, orange juice and rind. Add remaining ingredients, mixing well. Roll onto lightly floured board 1/2 cm (1/4") thickness. Cut into desired shapes place on cookie sheets, lightly greased. Sprinkle lightly with additional sugar and bake. Remove from cookie sheet to cool.

Bake: 160° (325°)
Time: 12-15 min.
Yield: 5 dozen

Welsh Cakes

Wonderful currant filled tea cakes

M.	Imp.	
125 gm	1/2 c	butter
125 ml	1/2 c	sugar
2	2	eggs
5 ml	1 t	vanilla
500 ml	2 c	flour
5 ml	1 t	baking powder
5 ml	1 t	nutmeg
2 ml	1/2 t	salt
75 ml	1/3 c	currants

Beat butter and sugar, add eggs and vanilla. Add remaining ingredients and mix well. Roll on a lightly floured board to a generous 1/2 cm (1/4"). Cut into rounds 7 cm size (2 1/2"). Place in a preheated electric fry pan until golden, turn and cook until golden on the other side.

Bake: 190° (375°)
Time: about 8 min.
Yield: 2 dozen

Jam-Jams

Delicious jam filled sandwich cookies

M.	Imp.	
75 ml	5 T	Roger's Golden syrup
250 ml	1 c	sugar
125 gm	½ c	butter or margarine
2	2	eggs
5 ml	1 t	vanilla
10 ml	2 t	baking soda
2 ml	½ t	salt
875 ml	3½ c	flour

raspberry jam

Beat until light and thoroughly combined the syrup, sugar, butter, eggs and vanilla. Add the baking soda, salt and flour; mix well. Roll to ½ cm (¼") on a lightly floured board. Cut into 7 cm (2½") rounds. Make a thimble sized hole in the centre of half of them to become the top rounds; the other half left plain are for the bottoms. Bake. Cool completely before filling with raspberry jam using a bottom and top round for each jam-jam. Best served next day (Freeze before filling for long keeping)

Bake: 180° (350°)
Time: 10-12 min
Yield: 30 sandwiches

Half Moons
A miniature fruit turnover

m	Imp	
125 gm	½ c	shortening
250 ml	1 c	sugar
1	1	egg
125 ml	½ c	milk
750 ml	3 c	flour
5 ml	1 t	baking soda
10 ml	2 t	baking powder
2 ml	½ t	salt

Combine in the given order. Roll out on a lightly floured surface to scant ½ cm (⅛"). Cut into 7 cm (2½") rounds. Fill with 5 ml (1 t.) filling and fold in half. Press edges with fork tines to seal. Place on baking sheet lightly greased and bake. Remove from oven and sprinkle lightly with sugar if desired

Fruit Filling

175 ml	3/4 c	raisins
175 ml	3/4 c	chopped dates
175 ml	3/4 c	water

Boil until thickened 5-10 min and cool.

Bake : 180° (350°)
Time: 10-15 min
Yield: 4½ dozen

Cookie Clues

Best results are obtained by:
- having all ingredients at room temperature
- using only top quality ingredients
- baking a sample cookie first if the recipe is new to you. That way you can check to see how much the cookie spreads and timing.
- remembering baking times are only approximate. Oven temperatures can vary greatly. You may wish to check your oven temperature with an oven thermometer for accuracy if times vary with those in this book
- allowing the heat to circulate freely in the oven. Baking sheets should be about 5 cm (2") smaller all around than your oven
- transferring cookies immediately to cooling racks
- cooling cookies completely before storing
- storing each kind of cookie separately. Soft cookies require a tight fitting lid; crisp cookies a loose fitting lid. Cookies freeze well.

Did you know that.... ?

- refrigerator cookie dough can be left overnight, several days and even frozen
- cookie batter if tightly covered will keep up to several days in the refrigerator
- nuts are best stored in the freezer
- yields are only approximate. Cookies can be made as small or as large as you choose. Adjust baking times accordingly
- frosted cookies will store best if laid without overlapping between layers of wax paper
- sifting flour is not necessary for the recipes in this book

All of the recipes in this book have been tested in our home. Many have also been tested with metric equipment (with equal success) based on the following chart

1 ml	· 1/4 t		50 ml	· 1/4 c
2 ml	· 1/2 t		75 ml	· 1/3 c
5 ml	· 1 t		125 ml	· 1/2 c
7 ml	· 1 1/2 t		150 ml	· 2/3 c
15 ml	· 1 T		175 ml	· 3/4 c
30 ml	· 2 T		250 ml	· 1 c
45 ml	· 3 T			

Books in the Just Series

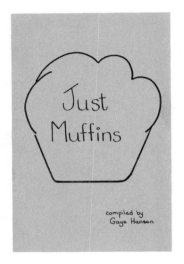

Just
Muffins

compiled by
Gaye Hansen

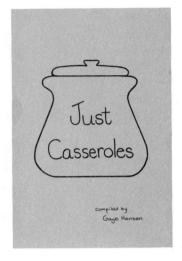

Just
Casseroles

compiled by
Gaye Hansen

Just
for
Tea

compiled by
Gaye Hansen

Just
Cookies

compiled and tested
by
Gaye Hansen